The Prayer Practice

A Four-Session Guide to Praying as Jesus Prayed

WaterBrook

John Mark Comer and Practicing the Way

WaterBrook
An imprint of the Penguin Random House Christian Publishing
Group, a division of Penguin Random House LLC
1745 Broadway, New York, NY 10019
waterbrookmultnomah.com
penguinrandomhouse.com

A WaterBrook Trade Paperback Original

Published in association with Yates & Yates, www.yates2.com.

Originally self-published by Practicing the Way
(practicingtheway.org) in 2023.

All photos courtesy of Practicing the Way.

Trade Paperback ISBN 978-0-593-60331-4
Ebook ISBN 978-0-593-60332-1

Printed in the United States of America on acid-free paper

1st Printing

Book and cover design by Practicing the Way.

For details on special quantity discounts for bulk purchases,
contact specialmarketscms@penguinrandomhouse.com.

The authorized representative in the EU for product safety
and compliance is Penguin Random House Ireland,
Morrison Chambers, 32 Nassau Street, Dublin D02 YH68,
Ireland. https://eu-contact.penguin.ie

Contents

PART 01

Getting Started

Welcome

Welcome to the Prayer Practice. You may have come on this Practice because you're new to following Jesus and learning to pray for the very first time. Or you may be at a stage in your apprenticeship to Jesus where you desire to not just learn about God, but to experience God. Or you may just find prayer boring or tedious, but you have a growing sense there's something you've yet to discover.

Whatever your motivation, we're so happy you've chosen to go on this four-session journey into a deeper life with God. In the hurry, distraction, and noise of the modern world, few things are more difficult, or more rewarding, than developing a life of prayer.

Prayer is simply the medium through which we communicate and commune with God. The practice of prayer is learning to set aside dedicated time to intentionally be with God in order to become like him and partner with him in the world.

When you are first learning to pray, there is a bit of a progression from one stage to the next. But the spiritual journey is not a linear progression, and you never mature beyond any dimension of prayer. This means we can revisit and grow within every layer many times.

As you give yourself to Jesus through this Practice, please remember: The ultimate aim is not to "pray more" or "pray better." It's what ancient Christians called union with God. As Julian of Norwich said long ago, "The whole reason why we pray is to be united into the vision and contemplation of him to whom we pray." It's to live each day more and more aware of and deeply connected to our Father; to be transformed into the likeness of his Son, Jesus; and to be filled with the fullness of his Spirit, to do what he made you to do in the world.

The Nine Practices

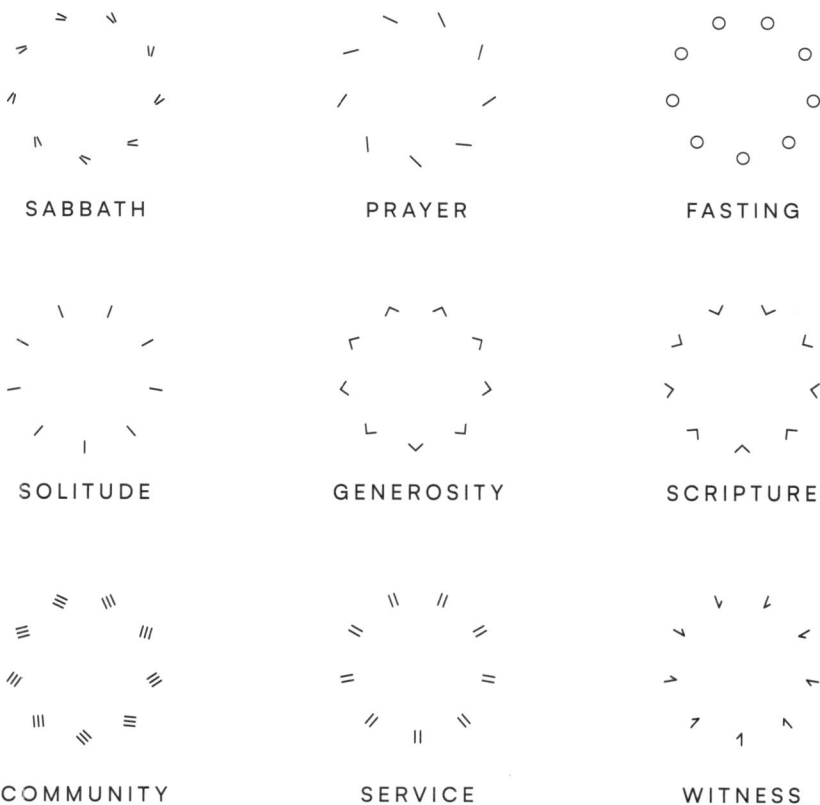

SABBATH

PRAYER

FASTING

SOLITUDE

GENEROSITY

SCRIPTURE

COMMUNITY

SERVICE

WITNESS

Prayer is just one of nine core Practices in the body of resources available from Practicing the Way. The Practices are spiritual disciplines centered around the life rhythms of Jesus. They are designed not to add even more to your already overbusy life, but to slow you down and create space for the Spirit of God to form you to be with Jesus, become like him, and do what he did. Ultimately, they are a way to experience the love of God.

To run another Practice or learn more, turn to page 108.

How to Use This Guide

A few things you need to know

This Practice is designed to be done in community, whether with a few friends around a table, within your small group, in a larger class format, or with your entire church.

The Practice is four sessions long. We recommend meeting together every week or every other week. For those of you who want to spend more time on this Practice, we've included an additional four weeks of bonus conversations in the appendix to go deeper in Scripture and discussion. You are welcome to pause for these conversations in between sessions or skip over them.

You will all need a copy of this Companion Guide. You can purchase a print or ebook version from your preferred retailer or find a free digital PDF version at launch.practicingtheway.org. We recommend the print version so you can stay away from your devices during the Practices, as well as take notes during each session. But we realize that digital works better for some.

Each session should take about one to two hours, depending on how long you allow for discussion and whether or not you begin with a meal. See the sample session on the following page.

Are you a group leader or facilitator? Log in to your online Dashboard or sign up at launch.practicingtheway.org to find ideas, best practices, and tips on running this Practice. Page 112 also offers helpful information and tips on running this Practice.

Our Practices are designed to work in a variety of group sizes and environments. For that reason, your gatherings may include additional elements like meals or worship time, or may follow a structure slightly different from the following sample. Please adapt as you see fit.

Sample Session

Here is what a typical session could look like.

Welcome

Welcome the group and open in prayer.

Share a meal (60 min.)

Gather around a table to eat together and share a conversation.

Introduction (2–3 min.)

Watch the introduction to the session and pause the video when indicated for your first discussion.

Discussion 01: Practice reflection in triads (15–20 min.)

Process your previous week's spiritual exercise in smaller groups of three to five people with the questions in the Guide.

Teaching (20 min.)

Watch the teaching portion of the video.

Discussion 02: Group conversation (15–30 min.)

Pause the video when indicated for a group-wide conversation.

Testimony and tutorial (5–10 min.)

Watch the rest of the video.

Prayer to close

Close by praying the liturgy in the Guide, or however you choose.

The Weekly Rhythm

The four sessions of this Practice are designed to follow a four-part rhythm that is based on our model of spiritual formation.

Learn
about the Way of Jesus.

IN COMMUNITY

Practice
with spiritual exercises using your Companion Guide.

WEEKLY   RHYTHM

Process together
what is coming up for you through your experience.

Reflect
on your experience with God.

ON YOUR OWN

01 Learn

Gather together as a community for an interactive experience of learning about the Way of Jesus through teaching, storytelling, and discussion. Bring your Guide to the session and follow along.

02 Practice

On your own, before the next session, go and "put it into practice,"* as Jesus himself said. We will provide weekly spiritual exercises to integrate this practice into your everyday life, as well as recommended resources to go deeper.

03 Reflect

Reflection is key to spiritual formation. After your practice and before the next session, set aside 10–15 minutes to reflect on your experience. Reflection questions are included in this Guide at the end of each session.

04 Process together

When you come back together, watch the introduction, and then start by sharing your reflections with your group. This moment is crucial because we need one another to process our lives before God and make sense of our stories. If you are meeting in a larger group, you will need to break into smaller subgroups for this conversation so everyone has a chance to share.

_____

* Ph lippians 4v9.

Tips on Beginning a New Practice

This Guide is full of spiritual exercises, time-tested strategies, and good advice on prayer as a spiritual practice.

But it's important to note that the Practices are not formulaic. We can't use them to control our spiritual formation or even our relationship with God. Sometimes they don't even work very well. Over the coming weeks, there may be some days when you experience God drawing near and speaking to you in prayer, and others when you just feel bored or distracted. That's normal.

The key with the spiritual disciplines is to let go of outcomes and just offer them up to Jesus in love.

Because it's so easy to lose sight of the ultimate aim of a Practice, here are a few tips to keep in mind as you practice prayer.

01 Start small

Start where you are, not where you "should" be. It's counterintuitive, but the smaller the start, the better chance you have of really sticking to it and growing over time.

If 30 minutes a day is too much, start with 10. If 10 is too much, start with five.

02 Think subtraction, not addition

Please do not add a daily prayer rhythm into your already overbusy, overfull life. Think, *What can I cut out?* A morning glance at the news? A lunch break scroll through social media? An evening TV-show habit?

Formation is about less, not more. About slowing down and simplifying your life around what matters most: life with Jesus.

03 You get out what you put in

The more fully you give yourself to this Practice, the more life-changing it will be; the more you just dabble with it, the more shortcuts you take, the less of an effect it will have on your transformation.

04 Remember the J curve

Experts on learning tell us that mastering a new skill tends to follow a J-shaped curve; we tend to get worse before we get better. If you currently enjoy your times of prayer, don't be surprised if some of these new types of prayer feel awkward and difficult. That's okay—it will get easier in time. Just stay with the Practice and see what it has to offer you.

05 There is no formation without repetition

Spiritual formation is slow, deep, cumulative work that takes years, not weeks. The goal of this four-session experience is just to get you started on a journey of a lifetime. Upon completion of this Practice, you will have a map for the journey ahead and hopefully some possible companions for the Way.

But what you do next is up to you.

Before You Begin

The following resources are designed to enhance your experience of the Prayer Practice, but they are entirely optional.

Recommended reading

Reading a book alongside the Practice can greatly enhance your understanding and enjoyment of prayer. You may love to read, or you may not. For that reason, it's recommended but certainly not required.

The recommended reading for the Prayer Practice is *Praying Like Monks, Living Like Fools* by Tyler Staton.

Tyler Staton is the lead pastor of Bridgetown Church in Portland, Oregon.

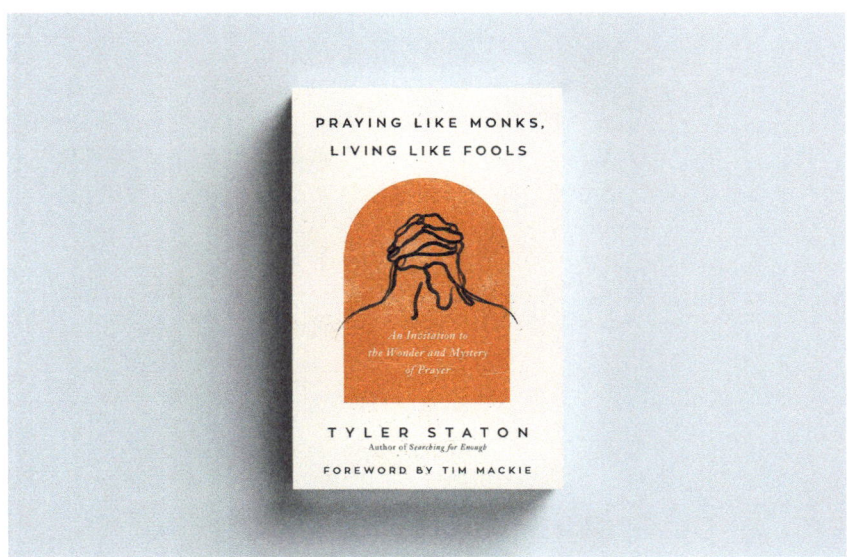

The Spiritual Health Reflection

One final note: Before you begin Session 01, please set aside 20—30 minutes and take the Spiritual Health Reflection. This is a self-assessment we developed in partnership with pastors and leading experts in spiritual formation. It's designed to help you reflect on the health of your soul in order to better name Jesus' invitations to you as you follow the Way.

You can come back to the Spiritual Health Reflection as often as you'd like (we recommend one to two times a year) to chart your growth and continue to move forward on your spiritual journey.

To access the Spiritual Health Reflection, visit practicingtheway.org/reflection and create an account. Answer the prompt questions slowly and prayerfully.

The Practicing the Way primer

If this is your first time engaging with a Practicing the Way resource, we invite you to set aside 15 minutes before Session 01 to watch a primer on spiritual formation. This will give you a brief overview of the *why* behind spiritual practices and key insights to guard and guide your coming practice.

Log in to your online Dashboard, or sign up to watch the primer at launch.practicingtheway.org.

PART 02

The Sessions

Talking to God

Overview

In Session 01, we explore the first stage of prayer: talking to God. When the disciples said to Jesus in Luke 11, "Teach us to pray," Jesus replied, "When you pray, say: 'Father, hallowed be your name...' " He gave them a premade prayer, or what some call a liturgy, to pray to God.

Liturgies can look like praying the Lord's Prayer, singing through the Psalms, or using a prayer app on your phone. This way of praying can be incredibly helpful in various seasons of our lives: when we're learning to pray, when we're exhausted or sick, when we're traveling and find it hard to focus, or when we're living with grief and doubt, searching for the right words to talk to God. "The prayers of the saints," as some call them, can carry us through.

So we start our four-session journey simply, by praying premade prayers to God.

This week's Practice will focus on the pragmatics of prayer. One of the single most important tasks of discipleship to Jesus is starting, habituating, and fine-tuning a daily prayer rhythm. Your daily prayer can be simple and brief. Yet it's as essential as sleeping, eating, and drinking. This is what will keep you praying in the days, months, and years to come.

Ronald Rolheiser writes:

> What clear, simple, and brief rituals provide is precisely prayer that depends upon something beyond our own energy. The rituals carry us, our tiredness, our lack of energy, our inattentiveness, our indifference, and even our occasional distaste. They keep us praying even when we are too tired to muster up our own energy.*

---

* "Sustaining a Prayer Life," Ron Rolheiser, accessed April 8, 2025, at ronrolheiser.com/sustaining-a-prayer-life/.

Opening Questions

When instructed, circle up in triads (smaller groups of three to five people) and discuss the following questions:

01 What emotions does the word *prayer* elicit in your heart?

02 What challenges do you face in prayer?

03 What invitation do you sense from God to go deeper in prayer?

Teaching

Key Scripture

Luke 11v1–4

Session summary

- Prayer is the medium through which we communicate and commune with God.

- The practice of prayer is learning to set aside dedicated time to intentionally be with God in order to become like him and better partner with him to do his work in the world.

- While for Jesus prayer seemed less like a discipline and more like a delight, for many of us, that is not our experience.

- We live in one of the most difficult times in human history to pray, given the distractions of the digital world, materialism, and secularism.

- Jesus teaches his disciples to pray the Lord's Prayer:*

  - "Our Father"—God is our Father.
  - "In heaven"—God is as close as the air.

  - "Hallowed be your name"— The first goal of prayer is the worshipful enjoyment of our Father's company.

  - "Your kingdom come, your will be done, on earth as it is in heaven"—Our prayers make a difference.

- Jesus teaches us to pray through the first-century Jewish custom of praying premade prayers. Examples of these premade prayers include:

  - The Lord's Prayer
  - Scripture
  - Songs
  - Liturgy

- Apps like Lectio 365 from 24-7 Prayer or Echo Prayer

- Prayer is the daily opening of our hearts to God, and whether it feels like much is "happening" or not—something is happening.

---

* Matthew 6v9–13.

Teaching Notes

As you watch Session 01 together, feel free to use this page to take notes.

Discussion Questions

Now it's time for a conversation about the teaching. Pause the video for a few minutes to discuss these questions in small groups:

01   What stuck out to you from that teaching?

02   Are premade prayers a part of your life with God? If not, how could they be?

03   What support do you need from this community as we go on this journey with God?

Practice Notes

As you continue to watch Session 01 together, feel free to use this page to take notes.

Closing Prayer

Take a few deep breaths, become aware of God's presence, and pray this prayer slowly, leaving a short silence between each line.

Open our hearts and minds, Father,

to the prayers of your Son and his saints,

to the guides who have long prayed before us,

to the movements of your Spirit in the rituals

and rhythms that have held those before us,

for the glory and affection of your name.

Amen.

Here are a few questions to hold in your mind as we enter this week's practice.

01 When will I pray?

First thing in the morning? After your workout? At night? On your lunch break? When the kids are napping? Many people find first thing in the morning to be best, but not always. As a general rule, give God your best time of day, when you are most awake and aware.

02 Where will I pray?

Most of us find it incredibly helpful to choose a dedicated space for prayer—a room in our home, a corner in our bedroom, a park bench near our house, or a literal prayer closet. This place can become a kind of modern-day altar, where you go to open up to God. Not because God hears us better at an altar, but because we hear God better!

03 How should I pray?

What posture is best for you? Sitting on a chair, a couch, or the floor? Kneeling? Standing? Walking? Lying down? Out loud or quiet? Does it help to begin with deep breathing first? How do you get your body to work with your heart's desire for God, not against it?

04 How long should I pray?

There's no "right" answer (to this or any of the other questions), but as a general rule, pray long enough to become present to God. And that may take a bit longer than you expect. If you have a newborn child or other extenuating circumstances that make 30 minutes too hard, that's fine. Start where you are, and take the next step forward in your journey.

In general, if we can't pray for 30 minutes a day, we're simply too busy. We need to take a serious life audit of what we believe is most important to us. After all, we're not trying to layer on more Christian busyness to our already over-maxed lives; we're trying to slow down and simplify our lives around what we most deeply desire—God.

Exercise

Part 01: Create a daily prayer rhythm.

Decide on a time and a place to pray, if possible, every day this week.

Decide on and commit to a time duration. Don't overreach. Start where you are. If you don't currently pray daily, aim for 10–15 minutes. If you currently pray for 10–15 minutes, consider upping it to half an hour. Just take the next step.

Create routines or rituals you actually enjoy to make your daily prayer habit something you look forward to all day long—light a candle, make yourself coffee or tea, sit by a window you love, go outside, savor the quiet, or put on worship music.

Those of you who are more kinesthetic may find it helpful to pray while walking, inside or in nature, or with something to keep your hands busy, like knitting or drawing.

Ultimately, work with your personality, not against it.

Write your plan here.

Part 02: Pick out a premade prayer, and talk to God.

Try using one of the sources we mentioned earlier.

- The Lord's Prayer

- The Psalms—See below for recommendations.

- Scripture—Find a passage that resonates with your heart, and pray it back to God.

- Songs—Sing a cappella, put on a worship album, or play an instrument.

- Liturgy—Read from the Book of Common Prayer, *The Divine Hours* by Phyllis Tickle, or *Every Moment Holy* by Douglas Kaine McKelvey.

- Apps—Download Echo, Lectio 365 from 24-7 Prayer, Pray As You Go from the Jesuits, or Hallow.

If you don't have a strong preference, we recommend you start by praying the Psalms or one of the prayers in the appendix of this Companion Guide.

You can start in Psalm 1 and pray through the book. Or you can pray a psalm based on your emotional or spiritual state that day.

Here are some recommendations.

- **To begin your day with God:** Psalm 5, 19, 20, 23, 25

- **When you are sad:** Psalm 13, 22, 42, 77

- **When you are in distress:** Psalm 57, 60, 86

- **When you are scared:** Psalm 27

- **When you are hurt:** Psalm 10

- **When you ache for more of God:** Psalm 63, 84

- **When you want to repent:** Psalm 51

- **When you are grateful:** Psalm 9, 103

- **When you want to worship:** Psalm 8, 148, 149, 150

Whatever you decide, pray at least once a day.

Circle or write what you feel led to try.

Reach Exercise

We recognize that we're all at different stages of discipleship and seasons of life. To that end, we've added a Reach Exercise to each of the four sessions for those who have the time, energy, and desire to go further in the Prayer Practice.

Follow the Lord's Prayer as a template.

This week's Reach Exercise is to utilize the Lord's Prayer as a template for a longer time of prayer by praying through each line. This should take around 15 minutes to pray, but feel free to take it at your own pace, listening to the Spirit's prompting.

You can do this exercise alone or as a group.

Follow this video tutorial from Strahan Coleman that will guide you step-by-step using prayer prompts: practicingtheway.org/pray-lordsprayer.

Or you can follow this written tutorial.

- To begin, find somewhere quiet. Put away your phone and any other distractions, and get into a comfortable but alert position.

- Take a few deep, slow breaths. Become aware of your surroundings, the sounds, how your body is today. Open up to God in this present moment.

- Then, praying from what you imagine or feel is a deep place within you, pray like this:

"Our Father..."

Think about the idea of God as your loving Parent, one who has good and kind intentions toward you. If you like, imagine him embracing you or smiling at you. Picture his face. Make eye contact with him.

"In heaven..."

Think about the idea that God is all around you. Like oxygen, he surrounds and soaks your body, his Spirit abiding within you. As you breathe, imagine that each breath invites God deeper into you. Remember that God loves living here, in you.

"Hallowed be your name..."

Sit with your Father in joyful, grateful worship. You might want to sit in silence for a few moments. Or sing a chorus. Or rattle off a list of things you're grateful for. Or praise God with specific things you love about him. You may just want to imagine your whole self being caught up into his, and what it feels like to be mingled with the God of love.

If you are in a group, encourage people to express their praise and gratitude out loud, one at a time. (For example, "Father, thank you for your kindness." "Father, thank you for loving me.")

"Your kingdom come, your will be done, on earth as it is in heaven..."

As you experience God's heart, allow it to inspire prayer for your city/church/community/life. Pray from this place of parental love. Allow the Spirit to lead you toward people, places, and situations that he longs to deliver, heal, and provide for. This type of prayer is referred to as intercession.

If you don't have a sense of God's leading, that's okay. Think of specific things you're aware of in your life and others' lives to pray for.

If you're in a group, one at a time, spend time verbally giving to God specific things in your life that you're wrestling with control over. A simple prayer of "Your will be done in _____" is a great place to start.

"Give us today our daily bread..."

Now spend some time asking God for things you need. Remembering that God is your Father, bring to him the provision, healing, and understanding you need, asking him to intervene. Your daily bread may be physical, relational, financial, emotional, or spiritual. Think of all the places you need him, inviting him to arrive there.

If you are in a group, do this with each person praying silently, out loud one at a time, or all together at once.

"Forgive us our debts, as we also have forgiven our debtors..."

Knowing that God sees you and longs to heal every part of you, spend a few minutes now in quiet asking God for forgiveness in specific areas. You can do that by speaking out loud the specific areas of sin and shame in your life, or by asking the Spirit to search your heart and reveal them to you.

Once you're done, ask the same for those who have sinned against you, asking the Spirit to help you continue to forgive them, releasing them to God.

If you are in a group, break into groups of two to three to confess sin to each other, only as you feel comfortable, or sit in a few moments of silence together.

"And lead us not into temptation, but deliver us from the evil one."

Ask for God's strength and resolve to resist temptation in the three enemies of your soul: the World, the Flesh, and the Devil. The World: its ideologies, consumerism and materialism, promiscuity, escapism, addiction, and greed. The Flesh: its pride, self-gratification, lust, and prejudice. The Devil: his lies, shaming, hatred, violence, and accusing.

Ask the Spirit to save you from giving in to the temptation of all three, even from what you're unable to see in your life. Ask for God's positive blessings in these spaces, inviting his goodness to lead the way and make itself evident in your every moment.

"For yours is the kingdom and the power and the glory, forever. Amen."

Take a moment to verbally declare the reality of this in your own language, attributing with love all glory to God in your body, your life, and the world around you.

Finish with a prayer of thankfulness and gratitude for God's presence with you during this time.

Practice Reflection

Reflection is a key component in our spiritual formation.

Millennia ago, King David prayed in Psalm 139v23–24:

> Search me, God, and know my heart;
>   test me and know my anxious thoughts.
> See if there is any offensive way in me,
>   and lead me in the way everlasting.

South African professor Trevor Hudson has quoted one of his pastoral supervisors as saying, "We do not learn from experience; we learn from reflection upon experience."*

If you want to get the most out of this Practice, you need to do it and then reflect on it.

_____

* Trevor Hudson, *A Mile in My Shoes: Cultivating Compassion* (Upper Room Books, 2005), 57.

Before your next time together with the group for Session 02, take 10–15 minutes to journal your answers to the following three questions:

01 Where did I feel resistance?

02 Where did I feel joy?

03 Where did I most experience God's nearness?

Note: As you write, be as specific as possible. While bullet points are just fine, if you write your insights out in narrative form, your brain will be able to process them in a more lasting way.

Reflection Notes

Keep Growing (Optional)

The following resources were created to enhance your experience of this Practice, but they are entirely optional.

📖 Read

Praying Like Monks, Living Like Fools by Tyler Staton (Chapters 01–03)

ᛁᛁᛁ Listen

Rule of Life podcast on prayer (Episode 01)
Join John Mark for a conversation with Reward Sibanda, Gemma Ryan, and Tyler Staton.

💬 Bonus Conversation

If you would like to slow down this four-week Practice to give your community more time to sit in each week's teaching and spiritual exercise, you can pause and meet for an optional conversation outlined in the appendix.

Talking with God

Overview

In Session 02, we begin to learn how to talk with God. Praying premade prayers is a beautiful way to pray. It's where we start our prayer journey, and it's a place we revisit all through our lives. But at some point in our life of prayer, we each desire to pray our own words to God—to share what's on our mind, our heart. Our pain, our joy, our hopes, and our fears. We can't help but desire to interact with God in a more authentic, personalized way.

We break down this next stage of prayer into three subcategories.

01   **Gratitude**—talking with God about what is good in your life and world

02   **Lament**—talking with God about what is evil in your life and world

03   **Petition and intercession**—asking God to fulfill his promises to overcome evil with good

Each one of these three dimensions of talking with God is like a vast territory we can explore for a lifetime and yet never see in its entirety.

Reflection Questions

When instructed, circle up in triads (smaller groups of three to five people) and discuss the following questions:

01   Where did you feel resistance in prayer?

02   Where did you feel delight?

03   Where did you most experience God's nearness?

Teaching

Key Scripture

Luke 11v5—13

Session summary

Gratitude is talking with God about what is good in your life and world.

- Generosity is at the center of the Gospel and God's nature, making gratitude the primary way we relate to God.

- Gratitude isn't just the beginning of prayer; it's the heart of our entire relationship with God.

- Our spiritual maturity can be measured by our level of gratitude.

Lament is talking with God about what is evil in your life and world.

- Two-thirds of the Psalms are lament.

- We are invited to pray what is in us, including pain, be it anger, grief, or jealousy.

- Lament is an emotionally healthy way of processing pain with God.

Petition and intercession is asking God to fulfill his promises to overcome evil with good.

- Petition is when we ask God to do something on our behalf, and intercession is when we ask God to do something on someone else's behalf.

- When we ask in prayer, we are to:
  - Ask in Jesus' name—as those in Christ and in alignment with Christ.
  - Ask like children—as those who are dependent.
  - Keep on asking—always pray, and do not give up.

- While the kingdom of God's will is not yet fully here, prayer makes a difference in what does—or does not—happen.

Teaching Notes

As you watch Session 02 together, feel free to use this page to take notes.

Discussion Questions

Pause the video for a few minutes and gather in small groups.

This week, instead of discussion, we invite you to pause and pray together.

Whether this is praying one at a time "popcorn" style or out loud all at once, we recommend you spend a few minutes on each of the categories of prayer from the teaching:

01   Gratitude

02   Lament

03   Petition and intercession

When you have finished those three movements, you can read aloud the closing prayer for this session.

Practice Notes

As you continue to watch Session 02 together, feel free to use this page to take notes.

Closing Prayer

Take a few deep breaths, become aware of God's presence, and pray this prayer slowly, leaving a short silence between each line.

Holy Spirit, we long to speak with you,
to be guided by the aches and hopes
of your heart, and to have you work
powerfully in and through us in this world.
Give us faith and teach us how to pray,
that we may more deeply partner with
you in all our living.

Amen.

Exercise

Part 01: Fine-tune your daily prayer rhythm.

It can take a very long time to figure out your daily routine for prayer—where to pray, when, how long, etc. And it's a moving target in the different seasons of our lives. So we're always fine-tuning: What's working? What's not?

Here are two things to consider incorporating into what you started last week.

Find an aid to "transition" in and out of prayer.

- Think of this aid as a micro-ritual to begin and end your daily time. You could light a candle, sit in silence for a few minutes, take ten deep, slow breaths, go for a walk, or utilize music. It can be anything that helps you unhurry and re-center on God's presence.

Use your body in prayer.

- We have an embodied faith and a wandering mind, so posture matters a lot in prayer.

- Biblically, the most common way to pray is not sitting or even kneeling but standing up and lifting your hands. But you can also pray sitting on the floor, kneeling, lying face down, walking, or, like Jesus did, climbing a mountain!

- Different postures are more conducive to different types of prayer. For example, standing and lifting your hands is ideal for intercessory prayer. Kneeling or lying face down on the floor are fitting postures for confession, repentance, or surrender. Walking can be a great posture to unburden your heart to God. Sitting cross-legged on the floor or in a firm chair to aid deep breathing is very helpful for quiet, contemplative prayer. There's no "right" way. Just experiment with your body and your daily prayer rhythm.

Write down a micro-ritual and a posture or two you'd like to try.

Part 02: Begin and/or end your day with gratitude.

While there's no "right" way to practice gratitude, we encourage you to use your imagination and creativity to "give thanks in all circumstances."*

Here are a few ideas.

- Begin your daily prayer time by giving thanks for three gifts of the day.

- Give thanks during everyday moments like while you commute to work, take a shower, or walk your dog.

- Keep a gratitude journal.

- Write out three gratitudes on a small piece of paper each morning, and then carry them in your pocket all day long.

- Go around the table at dinner with your family, spouse, roommates, or community and say what you are thankful for.

However you do it, at least once a day, pause, and give thanks for at least three good things in your life.

What would you like to do? Try to get specific about how and when—what time of day—you'll give this a try.

---

* 1 Thessalonians 5v18.

Part 03: Ask.

Step into petition and intercession, and ask on behalf of yourself and others. We have two recommended exercises to do this.

Prayer cards

- Make a deck of index cards with names or situations at the top of each card (or you can do one card with the most important people and situations in your life). *We challenge you to consider including your enemies or those you are struggling to forgive, as praying for them can set your heart free to love them.*

- Flip through your cards and linger over each one for a few seconds to a few minutes, offering up specific prayers to our Father. Remember, generic prayers make it harder to see God's hand in your life.

"Pray the room"

- This is a form of imaginative prayer that combines intercession with waiting on and listening for God. The goal is to pray what the Spirit of Jesus is already wanting you to pray from deep within.

- Get to a quiet, distraction-free place if at all possible. Take five to ten deep, slow breaths.

- Close your eyes and imagine yourself in a room with the Father or Jesus. Take a moment to visualize the room. If no specific room takes shape in your mind, use your memory of a room you love and experience God in.

- Ask the Holy Spirit to bring into the room anyone or anything that he wants you to pray for. Wait and see what comes into your field of vision.

  - How do they look? Are they happy? Sad? Bruised? Tired? Scared? Lost? What else do you notice about their appearance or demeanor?

- Then, pray for that person. Make your intercession as specific as possible. You can pray whatever is on your heart for them, or ask the Holy Spirit for further insight into what to pray for them. If you don't know what to pray, just hold them before God with love.

- Consider reaching out to that person to check in or offer a word of encouragement or sense of God's heart for them.

Circle which exercise you'd like to try first.

Reach Exercise

Pray your own lament.

Praying lament is a deeply personal experience. This exercise has been designed to help you connect with your own feelings and experiences so you can freely express them to God. Don't feel like you need to go deep if you're not ready. Remember, honesty is where the real power is with lament, so try not to filter your emotions and words.

Follow this video tutorial from Strahan Coleman that will guide you step-by-step, using prayer prompts: practicingtheway.org/pray-lament.

Or you can follow this written tutorial.

01   **Become aware.** To start, make yourself comfortable and take a few deep breaths. Become aware of your surroundings: the sounds, the temperature, how your body is today. Open up to God.

02   **Focus on a feeling.** Let yourself feel your present emotional state, your difficult situations and griefs and losses. You may have a few in your life. See if you can bring into focus one of those emotions or situations that you're currently feeling hurt or angry about.

03   **Sit with it.** Sit with that feeling, without judging it or telling yourself it's good or bad. Just notice how it feels. Can you locate it in your body? Your gut? Chest? Back? Shoulders? What is it like to hold that within you?

04   **Bring it to God.** Now imagine holding it out in your hands as you stand before him, so you can both see it. Tell God exactly how you feel, without a filter, and allow God to feel what you feel in this moment, to acknowledge the pain and grief that exists. Be raw, honest, and vulnerable. Let God hear all that's in your heart. Remember, you're taking your pain to him, on a quest for deeper intimacy, not rebellion. And know that God can bear

it, and that he knows what it's like to hurt. Hebrews 4v15 tells us that God sympathizes with us. Give God consent to sympathize with your lament.

05   **Express your desires and needs.** Plead with God to act, to change what is, to redeem or vindicate or heal or save or fight on your behalf. Wrestle with God if you feel the permission to do so.

06   **Give God your trust.** Then, let go. You might want to say, "Even though I feel [insert your emotion or lament], you are good and I trust you with it." Or, "I trust you; help my lack of trust!" Or use the ending to Jesus' own prayer of lament, "Not my will, but yours be done."*

07   **Be still.** For a few minutes, be still before God and allow him to respond. You may feel a lightness or a peace, you may see a picture or hear a word in your mind or imagination, or you might not. Notice how you feel after letting God hear your lament. Whatever happens, allow God the opportunity to meet you in this moment.

08   **Give thanks.** Finally, take a moment to thank God for being with you in this space. For listening, and for caring.

Reminder: Start with where you are. As an alternative to this tutorial, you can simply pray one of the Psalms of Lament. Scholars have found that approximately two-thirds of the 150 psalms are prayers of lament.

Here are a few we recommend to pray: Psalms 10, 13, 22, 42, 74, 77

---

* Luke 22v42.

Practice Reflection

Before your next time together with the group for Session 03, take 10–15 minutes to journal your answers to the following three questions:

01 What aspect of last session's exercises was most difficult for me—gratitude, lament, or asking?

02 Do I have any stories of answered prayer? Or unanswered prayer?

03 Where did I most experience God's nearness?

Note: As you write, be as specific as possible. While bullet points are just fine, if you write your insights out in narrative form, your brain will be able to process them in a more lasting way.

Reflection Notes

Keep Growing (Optional)

The following resources were created to enhance your experience of this Practice, but they are entirely optional.

📖 Read

Praying Like Monks, Living Like Fools by Tyler Staton (Chapters 04–05)

ᵢₗᵢₗ Listen

Rule of Life podcast on prayer (Episode 02)
Join John Mark for a conversation with Reward Sibanda, Gemma Ryan, and Tyler Staton.

💬 Bonus Conversation

If you would like to slow down this four-week Practice to give your community more time to sit in each week's teaching and spiritual exercise, you can pause and meet for an optional conversation outlined in the appendix.

Listening to God

Overview

There comes a point in our relationship to God where we desire not to just speak to him, but to listen. To hear his voice. As Jesus said, "My sheep listen to my voice; I know them, and they follow me."* This is a Spirit-generated desire in the heart of a disciple of Jesus. It was said of Jesus' disciple Mary that she "sat at the Lord's feet listening to what he said."** This is the primary posture of a disciple of Jesus: sitting at his feet and listening.

But how do we hear God's voice? He doesn't speak in the ways we're used to. Yet he does speak in a variety of ways. Ultimately through Jesus, then Scripture, circumstances, desire, prophecy, dreams, visions, the "still, small voice," and more.

Learning to sift through all the "voices" in our heads and discern how God is speaking to us is a key task of discipleship. But learning to hear is just the beginning; learning to obey is the even greater task. Our intention must be to really listen to God, with hearts of loving surrender and trust.

In this week's exercises, we practice two ancient and time-tested ways of listening to God.

---

* John 10v27.

** Luke 10v39.

Reflection Questions

When instructed, circle up in triads (smaller groups of three to five people) and discuss the following questions:

01 Where did you feel resistance in prayer?

02 Where did you feel delight?

03 Where did you most experience God's nearness?

Teaching

Key Scripture

John 10v2–5

Session summary

- Discipleship to Jesus is an interactive, dynamic, living relationship that includes hearing his voice.

- For Jesus, to "listen and obey" is the single most important task in the whole of the spiritual life.

- While there is no formula, here are six ways we hear God's voice:

  01 **Jesus**—Hearing God's voice begins and ends with Jesus as "the Word."

  02 **Scripture**—Specifically through the slow, quiet, and prayerful reading of a short passage, also called *Lectio Divina.*

  03 **Circumstances**—Learning to discern how God is coming to you through events or non-events.

  04 **Desires**—Listening carefully and critically to the desires of your heart to discern God's voice.

  05 **Prophecy**—Opening your imagination up to God and waiting for a word from him through Scripture, a picture, or a vision.

  06 **Listening prayer**—Waiting quietly for God to speak to your mind and heart through "guided thought."

- Listening to God requires what the New Testament calls "discernment."

  ○ Discernment is a skill we develop over time by the work of the Spirit, in community.

  ○ Most of all, our ability to discern God's voice grows through long hours spent listening.

Teaching Notes

As you watch Session 03 together, feel free to use this page to take notes.

Discussion Questions

Now it's time for a conversation about the teaching. Pause the video for a few minutes to discuss these questions in small groups:

01   Have you ever tried to listen for God's voice before? If not, why not?

02   What fears or hopes does this type of prayer bring up in your heart?

03   What's the primary way that you hear God's voice in your life?

Practice Notes

As you continue to watch Session 03 together, feel free to use this page to take notes.

Closing Prayer

End your time together by praying this liturgy:

Help us, God, to build a listening life,
a life of quiet attentiveness, a life of
faith and receptivity, that we may
know you not only through what we're
told, but personally, frequently, in the
very center of our being.

Amen.

Exercise

Part 01: *Lectio Divina*

Lectio Divina is an ancient Latin phrase, first used by Saint Benedict in the sixth century. It means "spiritual reading." It's a way of reading Scripture slowly and prayerfully, listening for God's word to you. While you do not need to follow this four-step process, there are four movements to *Lectio Divina* that you may find helpful.

First, go somewhere quiet and as distraction-free as possible. Open your Bible and pick out a passage that's conducive to *Lectio*—a psalm, a portion of the Gospels, or a section of an epistle (another word for letter, such as Romans, Ephesians, Philippians, etc.). Take a few deep breaths. Then:

- **Read**—Take in a passage of your choice, slowly and prayerfully. Pay special attention to any words, phrases, or ideas that jump out to you or that deeply resonate or move you emotionally.

- **Reflect**—Reread the passage again, slowly. This time, pause over the word(s) or phrase(s) that were highlighted to you during your first reading. Meditate on them. Turn them over in your mind. Savor them.

- **Respond**—Pray your impressions back to God. You can use your own words or simply pray the text directly to God.

- **Rest**—Take a few minutes in silence to breathe deeply and rest in God's loving word to you.

Repeat this three to five times this coming week.

If you're doing this as a group, find somewhere quiet and distraction-free and read the four steps above out loud. Share your impressions with one another and pray them together to God.

Part 02: Listening prayer

First, go somewhere quiet and distraction-free. Then:

- **Breathe**—Take a minute or two to just breathe slowly and deeply, clearing your mind to receive God's word to you. You may want to simply pray, "Father," or, "Jesus," or, "Come, Holy Spirit," as you inhale and exhale each breath.

- **Be silent**—Ask God to silence the voice of the enemy in your mind, to clear the air around you, to shield and guard your imagination.

- **Ask the Spirit to speak to you.**

- **Open your mind and heart to listen.** First Corinthians 6v19 tells us our "bodies are temples of the Holy Spirit." The Spirit within you has direct access to your imagination. Wait quietly with a surrendered heart. He may come to you in a:

  - Word or phrase
  - Scripture
  - Thought
  - Metaphor
  - Picture in your mind
  - Short film, kind of a series of pictures in your mind
  - Feeling in your heart
  - Sensation in your body

If nothing comes, don't judge yourself, or God. Just give thanks for his love and try again later. Our job is to be present to God and to listen for his voice when he desires to speak to us.

Test whatever you "hear" against Scripture and in community.

Finally, if God's word to you was directional, obey. Go do what he said!

Reach Exercise

Pray the Examen.

This exercise, the Examen, was developed by Saint Ignatius of Loyola as a way of reviewing one's day with God. Saint Ignatius taught that God often speaks through our emotions and that, by becoming aware of them, we may also become aware of the Spirit's movements in our own lives. He also encouraged talking to Jesus as a friend, sitting with and sharing our lives with him. The Examen was designed as a regular practice for the end of the day or week.

Follow this video tutorial from Strahan Coleman that will guide you step-by-step, using prayer prompts: practicingtheway.org/pray-examen.

Or you can follow this written tutorial.

01   **Become aware of God.** Review the day with the eyes of the Holy Spirit, asking God for the light to see. It may seem rushed to you, a blur or chaotic. If you feel overwhelmed or struggle to focus, ask the Spirit to help you see and bring focus to your mind.

02   **Look back with gratitude.** As you explore your day, take note of moments where you can thank God for what's been. It may be as simple as noting the provision of food and waking in the comfort of your bed. Think about the people in your day and the connections made. Where was God in each relationship or conversation? Recall the little things about your day, simple everyday pleasures, and discover God among them.

03   **Notice your emotions**. Reflect on your feelings throughout the day. What do you notice? Without judging what you felt, did you feel anger? Contentment? Empathy? Happiness? Embarrassment? Trusting that God speaks through our emotions, what do you think God was saying amid them?

04   **Pray from one piece of your day.** Allowing the Holy Spirit to highlight one element of your day, be it positive or negative, ask him to speak to you about it. Consider it with him and allow it to lead you to prayer, whether it's gratitude, intercession, petition, repentance, or praise.

05   **Look ahead to tomorrow.** Finally, ask God to prepare your heart for tomorrow. Notice how you feel about it—anxious, excited, nervous, overwhelmed—and invite the Spirit to speak to those joys and concerns. Ask for clarity for the day ahead and for peace to approach it with confidence. Ask for wisdom, for hope, for discernment.

Practice Reflection

Before your next time together with the group for Session 04, take 10–15 minutes to journal your answers to the following three questions:

01   Where did I feel resistance?

02   Where did I feel delight?

03   As you sat with God, did the Spirit convict or comfort you in any area of your life?

Note: As you write, be as specific as possible. While bullet points are just fine, if you write your insights out in narrative form, your brain will be able to process them in a more lasting way.

Reflection Notes

Keep Growing (Optional)

The following resources were created to enhance your experience of this Practice, but they are entirely optional.

📖 Read

Praying Like Monks, Living Like Fools by Tyler Staton (Chapters 06–08)

⑴⑾⑴ Listen

Rule of Life podcast on prayer (Episode 03)
Join John Mark for a conversation with Reward Sibanda, Gemma Ryan, and Tyler Staton.

🗨 Bonus Conversation

If you would like to slow down this four-week Practice to give your community more time to sit in each week's teaching and spiritual exercise, you can pause and meet for an optional conversation outlined in the appendix.

Being with God

Overview

We never mature beyond any of the four stages of prayer we are exploring in this Practice, but the further we progress in prayer, the more we desire to speak to God, listen to God, and just be with God.

As a general rule, you can gauge the intimacy in a relationship by how comfortable you are being alone together in the silence. Early on, relationships are full of words and activity. As you grow closer over time, there are still words and activity, but you also come to deeply enjoy just being with each other.

In the later stages of prayer, all human metaphors fall short, but the most ancient metaphor for this stage is marriage. There is a level of intimacy in marriage that is the intermingling of persons at the deepest level. It is wordless, yet it is a form of communication and, more, communion. Followers of Jesus have long considered this sacred love to be a picture of union with God.

This type of wordless prayer has come to be called "contemplation," based on 2 Corinthians 3v18. Its most basic meaning is to contemplate: to look, to gaze upon the beauty of God, receiving his love pouring out toward you in Christ and by the Spirit, and then giving your love back in return.

In our final week's exercises, we explore this way of being with God in love.

Reflection Questions

When instructed, circle up in triads (smaller groups of three to five people) and discuss the following questions:

01 What was your experience of listening prayer like?

02 Did you sense God saying anything to you this week?

03 As you sat with God, did the Spirit convict or comfort you in any area of your life?

Teaching

Key Scripture

2 Corinthians 3v18

Session summary

- The further we progress in prayer, the more we will desire to talk with God and listen to him, but, even more, to simply be with him.

- This kind of wordless communion has come to be called contemplative prayer.

- The Singaporean writer Hwee Hwee Tan said, "You are what your mind looks at. You are what you contemplate."*

- Contemplative prayer has three basic dimensions:

  01 Looking—to look at God's beauty, goodness, and love pouring out toward you.

  02 Yielding—to let go of outcomes and surrender your will to God's presence and purposes.

  03 Resting—to experience and remain in God's love.

- We can expect three challenges in contemplative prayer:

  01 Distraction

  02 Hurry

  03 Our own inner turmoil

- In order to adopt a slower, more prayerful lifestyle, we can begin by arranging our lives around a daily prayer rhythm.

---

* Hwee Hwee Tan, "In Search of the Lotus Land," *Quarterly Literary Review Singapore* 1, no. 1 (October 2001), www.qlrs.com/essay.asp?id=140.

Teaching Notes

As you watch Session 04 together, feel free to use this page to take notes.

Discussion Questions

Now it's time for a conversation about the teaching. Pause the video for a few minutes to discuss these questions in small groups:

01 In what ways have you experienced glimpses of this kind of prayer with God?

02 How do you normally handle distraction when you pray?

03 How and where do you most sense God's withness in your life?

Practice Notes

As you continue to watch Session 04 together, feel free to use this page to take notes.

Closing Prayer

End your time together by praying this liturgy:

Teach us, in loving, unceasing
beholding love, to be with you, God, in our
affections, in our deepest places, in our
daily, ordinary living, that we may live in
grateful, unspoken communion with you,
relenting to your desire.

Amen.

Exercise

Begin your daily prayer rhythm with silence and a breath prayer.

The seventh-century monk Saint John Climacus gave this advice on contemplation: "Let the memory of Jesus combine with your breath." Contemplatives have long used the God-ordained process of breathing to attune to the breath/spirit/pnuema of God within the "temples" of their bodies. God has designed deep, slow breathing to calm your body's nervous system and center your mind. That makes breathing an especially helpful pathway to contemplative prayer.

Contemplative prayer is difficult because our minds are so distraction-prone, but the basic steps are simple.

- Find a quiet, distraction-free place to pray.

- Get seated comfortably, where you can breathe properly and not slouch. We recommend either using a dining chair with your feet on the floor and your back straight and shoulders upright, or sitting cross-legged directly on the floor, with a pillow or cushion under your backside to help with blood circulation. Not on a couch.

- Breathe slowly (five seconds on the inhale, then five on the exhale) from your belly. Relax. Become present to your body and to the moment. Then, open your mind to God.

- You may just want to remain here, in loving attention to the Trinity. Remember: You're not trying to pray words. It's your heart to God's heart; this prayer is will to will, love to love.

- Or you may want to combine a prayer word to your breath. A prayer word is simply a word or phrase that you use to keep your attention fixed on God.

  - Many use "Father" or "Abba" or "Jesus."

  - Others use a phrase from Scripture like "The Lord is my shepherd" (on the inhale), "I lack nothing" (on the exhale).

  - The Eastern church uses the Jesus Prayer: "Lord Jesus Christ" (on the inhale), "have mercy on me" (on the exhale).

  - You can also use your own phrase, like "In you I live" (on the inhale), "In you I delight" (on the exhale).

  - There's no "right" prayer word. It's just a tool to keep your wandering mind focused on God's presence within you.

- When distractions come, just gently set them aside the moment you realize your mind has wandered, and come back to your breathing and prayer word. And they will come, way more than you think or want! That's okay. It doesn't mean you're bad at contemplative prayer; it means you're human.

Remain in God, receiving his love and giving yours back in turn. In the beginning, one or two minutes of this is a huge success, and five to ten minutes is a home run.

Reach Exercise

Engage in the Beholding Prayer (the Window of the Soul).

This exercise—the Window of the Soul—is one way to practice beholding (or contemplative prayer). What's important is that we bring all of ourselves to God and allow him to be present to us with compassion, kindness, and love, setting our eyes on the God that is, and not the one we may assume or fear. It can take practice to become comfortable with this kind of prayer, so don't worry if you don't fully connect the first time. The most important part is our being lovingly available to God.

Follow this video tutorial from Strahan Coleman that will guide you step-by-step, using prayer prompts: practicingtheway.org/pray-beholding.

Or you can follow this written tutorial.

Note: For each step below, take a minute or two to sit and abide in the process.

01 **Become aware.** Make yourself comfortable and take a few deep breaths. Become aware of your surroundings—the sounds, the temperature, etc. How does your body feel today? Heavy, light, sore, calm? Reconnecting with yourself helps bring all of you to God in prayer.

02 **Sink into your heart.** Try and focus on where you feel the deepest within your body. It may be in your heart, your chest, or your belly. If you're not sure, try to imagine there is an elevator that descends from your head, through your neck, past your collarbone, and into your heart. Place those thoughts in the elevator and send them down into your heart. Don't deny them or try to get rid of them; just allow them to sink into your heart's center as you pray.

03 **Open yourself up to God.** While you're in that space, begin to open yourself up to God. If it's helpful, imagine that there are outward-opening French doors within you, where your soul feels most present. As you picture them, imagine opening those doors to God and offering him every part of who you are—the good, the not good, the celebrated, and the vulnerable or ashamed. Imagine having no part of you left hidden by choice from God. All is available to be seen.

04 **Look to God.** As you bring your whole self to him, look toward him. You might imagine Jesus' face, or you may simply look toward his loving presence. In John 15v9, Jesus said, "As the Father has loved me, so have I loved you." Allow yourself to see God gazing upon you with love, openness, compassion, and joy. Give him consent to reveal that love toward you personally. Imagine his gaze pouring through the doorway to your soul.

05 **Sit with God.** Without agenda, allow him to be however he longs to be with you. You may feel or see something beautiful. If not, this time is just as important. Let yourself just be open to God in whatever way today demands, allowing him to be with you. Notice how it feels to be fully seen by God and to be fully open toward him.

06 **Return to awareness.** As you finish your time together, take a moment to thank God for his love and for being present to you. Then, slowly come back into awareness of the sounds and sensations of the room around you.

Practice Reflection

As you come to the end of this Practice, take 10–15 minutes to journal your answers to the following three questions.

01   Where did I feel resistance?

02 Where did I feel delight?

03 Where did I most experience God's nearness?

Note: As you write, be as specific as possible. While bullet points are just fine, if you write your insights out in narrative form, your brain will be able to process them in a more lasting way.

Reflection Notes

Keep Growing (Optional)

The following resources were created to enhance your experience of this Practice, but they are entirely optional.

Read

Praying Like Monks, Living Like Fools by Tyler Staton (Chapters 09–10)

Listen

Rule of Life podcast on prayer (Episode 04)
Join John Mark for a conversation with Reward Sibanda, Gemma Ryan, and Tyler Staton.

Bonus Conversation

If you would like to slow down this four-week Practice to give your community more time to sit in each week's teaching and spiritual exercise, you can pause and meet for an optional conversation outlined in the appendix.

May Jesus teach you to pray—to commune and communicate with our Father—and lead you into a deeper life of union with the Spirit.

PART 03

Continue the Journey

You are not going to explore the vast territory of prayer in four sessions. This Practice is designed only to get you moving on a lifelong journey. The daily prayer rhythm you've been practicing is meant to be integrated into your Rule of Life and become the baseline for your life with God. But prayer is a journey in which we never "arrive," and there is always more.

Where you go from here is entirely up to you, but if you decide to integrate a daily prayer rhythm into your life, here's a list of next steps to continue your Practice.

Recommended Reading

Beholding by **Strahan Coleman**

A beautiful look at more contemplative ways of being with God and resting in his love.

Armchair Mystic by **Mark E. Thibodeaux**

One of the best overall books on prayer we've found, guiding you through the various layers of prayer.

A Praying Life by **Paul E. Miller**

A classic work on the power and discipline of petition and intercession. You will be deeply inspired to *ask*.

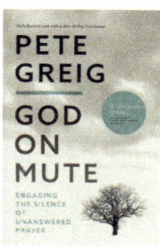

God on Mute by **Pete Greig**

An emotionally honest, theologically sound, and intellectually rich exploration of unanswered prayer and seasons of spiritual dryness and suffering.

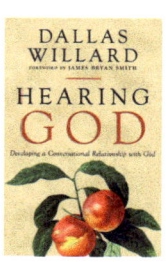

Hearing God by **Dallas Willard**

A thoughtful exploration of the theology, philosophy, and practice of learning to hear God's voice.

Prayer by **Richard J. Foster**

One of the best compilations on prayer ever written, this trusted spiritual guide works through pretty much all the various types of prayer in Christian spirituality.

Recommended Exercises

01 Practice Sabbath.

Most of us are simply too busy to pray. Sabbath is one of the most important disciplines for the spiritual life in our day, because it opens up time and space in our overcrowded lives to find our lifes in God. The practice of Sabbath is like a container for so many other practices.

The Sabbath Practice is available at practicingtheway.org/sabbath, but here are a few small steps to get started.

- Choose a day to Sabbath (or if a full 24 hours is too much, start with a half day or a few hours after church).
- Begin your Sabbath with some kind of small ritual to transition into Sabbath time—like lighting a candle, reading a psalm, or eating a meal with family or friends.
- Spend your Sabbath ceasing from all work, chores, buying, selling, and entertainment. In their place, give yourself to rest, delight, and worship.
- Run the Sabbath Practice, listen to the *Rule of Life* podcast Series One: Sabbath, and/or read a book about the Sabbath to continue to learn more about this ancient discipline for emotional health and spiritual life.

02 Go on retreat.

Find a monastery, retreat center, rural hotel, or vacation home and go away for an extended time of quiet, rest, Sabbath, and prayer. If going away isn't feasible in this season, eight hours is a great start and can expand over time. Two to three days would be harder but deeply impactful and worth working your way up to over the course of a few retreats.

The longer we give ourselves to solitude, silence, and stillness, the more space it opens up in us for healing and renewal in God.

03 Continue to develop a daily prayer rhythm.

We need to develop a rich life with God in our ordinary lives, not just on retreat or special occasions. Our daily rhythms of prayer are absolutely essential to our discipleship. The best place to start is by developing and fine-tuning your daily prayer rhythm, or what ancient Christians called the "Daily Office."

Once you've firmly established a daily prayer habit each morning (or whenever you decide is best for you to pray), begin to slowly expand.

Choose a second time and place to pause for another moment of daily prayer. If you pray in the morning, try stopping again after work and before dinner (when you're not too tired) or just before bed (if you're more of a night person). Or try praying on your lunch break or during a break in your daily routine of work, school, or caregiving. You may want to use your body differently: If you sit for morning prayer, try going on a walk or standing or kneeling.

Experiment with different types of prayer that meet different needs, like petition and intercession midday and the Examen at night (or whatever you discern is best).

When you get busy and fall out of your rhythm, don't judge yourself or feel bad; it's very normal. Just begin again.

Remember: The end goal is not to pray X number of times a day. It's to rearrange your daily life so you are experiencing deep joy, peace, and gratitude in your everyday life with God.

The Practices

Information alone isn't enough to produce transformation.

By adopting not just the teaching but also the practices from Jesus' own life, we open up our entire beings to God and allow him to transform us into people of love.

Our nine core Practices work together to form a Rule of Life for the modern era.

Sabbath	**Prayer**	**Fasting**
Solitude	**Generosity**	**Scripture**
Community	**Service**	**Witness**

WHAT'S INCLUDED FOR EACH PRACTICE

Four Sessions

Each session includes teaching, guided discussion, and weekly exercises to integrate the Practices into daily life.

Companion Guide

A detailed guide provides question prompts, session-by-session exercises, and space to write and reflect.

Recommended Resources

Additional recommended readings and podcasts offer a way to get the most out of the Practices.

Learn more by visiting practicingtheway.org/resources.

The Practicing the Way Course

An eight-session primer on spiritual formation.

Two thousand years ago, Jesus said to his disciples, "Follow me." But what does it mean for us to follow Jesus today?

The Practicing the Way Course is an on-ramp to spiritual formation, exploring what it means to follow Jesus and laying the foundation for a life of apprenticeship to him.

WHAT'S INCLUDED

Eight Sessions

John Mark and other voices teaching on apprenticing under Jesus, spiritual formation, healing from sin, meeting God in pain, crafting a Rule of Life, living in community, and more

Exercises

Weekly practices and exercises to help integrate what you've learned into your everyday life

Guided Conversations

Prompts to reflect on your experience and process honestly in community

Companion Guide

A detailed workbook with exercises, space to write and reflect, and suggestions for supplemental resources

Learn more by visiting practicingtheway.org/resources.

Practicing the Way:
Be with him. Become like him. Do as he did.

The first followers of Jesus developed a Rule of Life, or habits and practices based on the life of Jesus himself. As they learned to live like their teacher, they became people who made space for God to do his most transformative work in their lives.

Practicing the Way is a vision for the future, shaped by the wisdom of the past. It's an introduction to spiritual formation accessible to both beginners and lifelong followers of Jesus, and a companion to the Practicing the Way Course. This book offers theological substance, astute cultural insight, and practical wisdom for creating a Rule of Life in the modern age.

You can order your copy or get copies for your community at practicingtheway.org/book or through your preferred bookseller.

The Circle

Practicing the Way is a nonprofit that develops spiritual formation resources for churches and small groups learning how to become apprentices in the Way of Jesus.

We believe one of the greatest needs of our time is for people to discover how to become lifelong disciples of Jesus. To that end, we help people learn how to be with Jesus, become like him, and do as he did, through the practices and rhythms he and his earliest followers lived by.

All of our downloadable ministry resources are available at no cost, thanks to the generosity of The Circle and other givers from around the world who partner with us to see formation integrated into the church at large.

To learn more or join us, visit practicingtheway.org/give.

For Facilitators

Before you begin, there are three easy things you need to do (this should take only 10–15 minutes).

01   Go to launch.practicingtheway.org, log in, create a group, and send a digital invitation to your community. This will give your group access to the Spiritual Health Reflection, videos, and all sorts of valuable extras. Encourage your group to bring along their Companion Guides to each session, as these contain the discussion questions and space to take notes.

- You can purchase a print or ebook version from your preferred retailer or find a free digital PDF version at launch.practicingtheway.org. We recommend the print version so you can stay away from your devices during the Practices, as well as take notes during each session. But we realize that digital works better for some.

- Note: You can order the Guides ahead of time and have them waiting when people arrive for Session 01, or encourage people to order or download their own and bring them to your gatherings.

02   Send a message to your group encouraging everyone to take the Spiritual Health Reflection before your first gathering. You can direct your group to practicingtheway.org/reflection.

03   If your group has not been through the Practicing the Way Course, invite them to watch the short primer in the online Dashboard before you gather for Session 01 of this Practice.

For training, tips, and more resources for facilitating the Prayer Practice, log in to the Dashboard at launch.practicingtheway.org.

APPENDIX

Bonus Conversations

Talking to God

The Psalms have been the primary prayer book for Israel and the church throughout history, and even for Jesus of Nazareth himself. They are prayers that teach us to pray not with religious grandiosity but with humanity. Today's psalm is no exception. In it, we see the psalmist bearing their soul in prayer seemingly without a need to edit their questions or frustrations—even those directed at God. And while this kind of prayer might seem like it is in opposition to faith, the opposite is actually true. Prayers like these are a sign of a maturing faith that goes toward God in pain, not away from him. Praying like this is what moves us from the kinds of performative prayers that exhaust us toward an honest way of praying that can ultimately enliven us.

Read Psalm 42

Discuss the Scripture

01   What most stands out to you personally about this prayer?

02   This prayer is an example of lament—talking with God about pain in your life and the world. Do you gravitate toward or away from prayers like this? Why do you think that is?

03   How performative versus honest do you feel your prayers typically are? What permission does a prayer like this give you in your own prayer life?

04   One of the repeated lines in this psalm is "put your hope in God." In what areas of your life today are you finding it hard to do or pray this? What invitations do you sense there?

Discuss the practice

01   What does your daily prayer rhythm look like? What have you done to make it work with your personality, not against it?

02   What premade prayer did you select for this week's exercise? How was the experience of praying that for you?

03   Would you say you gravitate toward praying in this way or toward a more spontaneous life of prayer? What distinct value can you see, or have you experienced, in praying premade prayers?

04   What kind of expectations do you notice yourself bringing into your prayer time? How might those expectations need adjusting to better serve you?

Repeat the exercise

For this week, continue in your daily prayer rhythm from last week's exercise. Pay attention to how this rhythm feels for you, and consider how you might fine-tune it going forward. It's normal, out of excitement or ambition, to overreach in the plans we create around prayer and to need to adjust.

We also encourage you to integrate premade prayers into your daily prayer time. Take a look at the options provided starting on page 129, and either plan in advance which prayers you want to pray or have a few prepared to pray depending on your emotional or spiritual state that day.

Talking with God

It's normal if you find yourself wrestling not just with how to pray, but with what to pray. In today's Scripture, the author, Paul, speaks to the *what* of prayer with two simple words: "every situation." That might initially feel intimidating, but it's not meant to; it's meant to be liberating. According to Paul, we don't need to overthink what we pray; every context is the proper context for prayer.

But this text isn't just about processing with God—though it is that, too. It's also an invitation toward petition, or asking of God, and toward the belief that, in whatever you're facing, Jesus is proposing to you personally his famous question from the Gospels: "What do you want me to do for you?"* Paul assures us that as we enter into this honest and bold kind of prayer, our experience will be peace—the kind of peace that the nineteenth-century preacher Charles Spurgeon described as "the unruffled serenity of the infinitely-happy God, the eternal composure of the absolutely well-contented God."**

Read Philippians 4v6–7

Discuss the Scripture

01   In what aspect of this Scripture do you sense a deeper invitation?

02   How does thanksgiving typically show up in your life of prayer? Does it feel natural or unnatural to you?

03   What requests are you praying to God lately? What has been your experience as you have brought those requests to him?

04   What is one area in your life where you long for the kind of peace this Scripture talks about? How have you experienced this before?

---

* Mark 10v51.

** Charles Haddon Spurgeon, "Prayer, the Cure for Care," January 12, 1888, Metropolitan Tabernacle Pulpit Collection, vol. 40, The Spurgeon Center, www.spurgeon.org/resource-library/sermons/prayer-the-cure-for-care/#flipbook/.

Discuss the practice

01   How is your daily prayer rhythm going so far? What have you needed to subtract, add, or change along the way?

02   What have you noticed about how this daily time in prayer impacts the rest of your day?

03   How did you decide to integrate gratitude into your life of prayer? Do you see this practice affecting your outlook or perspective throughout the day? How so?

04   What have you found yourself asking God for in your own life or in the lives of others around you? How has this exercise shifted how you relate to your needs or the needs of others?

Repeat the exercise

For last week's exercise, you were invited to:

    01 Fine-tune your daily prayer rhythm.

    02 Begin and/or end your day with gratitude.

    03 Step into petition and intercession.

This week, referencing the exercise on page 54, practice the following:

- Reflect on your experience of adding new transitions or postures to your daily prayer rhythm. What's working? What's not working? What do you want to carry forward or adjust in this rhythm for the remainder of the Practice?

- Revisit the list of ideas for practicing gratitude. If the idea you chose felt helpful and suited you, keep practicing it. If you think you could benefit from adjusting to a different way of practicing gratitude, consider choosing one of the ideas on the list or coming up with an idea yourself.

Write your updated plan below, getting specific about how and when—what time of day—you'll give this a try.

For prayer and petition this week, choose one of the two recommended exercises provided—prayer cards or "pray the room"—and practice the one that you didn't try in the previous week.

Listening to God

To pray is to be distracted—this is the inevitable experience of every pray-er. The main question when it comes to distraction in prayer is not whether we will outgrow it, but how we will train ourselves to respond to it. The invitation is to return and keep returning to God in prayer, despite being distracted; to do what Thomas Keating describes: "If your mind gets distracted a thousand times in ten minutes of prayer, that's a thousand chances to come back to God." In today's story from *The Gospel of Luke*, the issue was not that Martha was hosting but that, in hosting Jesus, she became distracted from him and stayed distracted from him. Jesus' encouragement to all of us in the distracted place is to become like Mary when we feel like Martha: to return to listening at his feet. This is the cycle of discipleship: to sit, listen, obey, and then repeat, over and over again in the span of a lifetime.

Read Luke 10v38–42

Discuss the Scripture

01   What stands out to you personally from this story?

02   What distractions do you most commonly experience in your times of prayer? What feelings do those distractions elicit for you?

03   How often does your life of prayer consist of listening versus talking? What feels challenging and compelling about prayer becoming a two-sided conversation for you?

04   Jesus makes a profound statement about Mary's choice to be at His feet, saying that "few things are needed—or indeed only one." What do you think is so important to Jesus about Mary's posture? What insight does this give us into what Jesus most desires for us?

Discuss the practice

01 How do you typically read Scripture? In what ways was *Lectio Divina* different or similar to your usual approach to the Bible?

02 Reflecting on the last week of practicing *Lectio Divina*, what moment, impression from Scripture, or theme stands out to you the most?

03 Share about your time practicing listening prayer this past week. Was it uncomfortable? Impactful? Disappointing?

04 What kind of resistance or confusion did you experience in hearing God's voice? What has this experience taught you about how to approach or what to expect when discerning His voice?

Repeat the exercise

This week, continue to practice *Lectio Divina* during your time in Scripture and keep listening prayer integrated with your regular prayer times. It's important to remember that when trying out new practices like these, they can initially feel awkward or maybe even discouraging, depending on the expectations you had going into them. That's normal. We encourage you to stay with the practice and trust that God wants to speak to you personally in His Word and in prayer.

Being with God

Prayer is the lifeblood of our apprenticeship to Jesus. The practice of prayer is all about carving out intentional time to be with God, allowing that time to shape us to become more like him and partner with him in his work in the world. While these three elements that mark the life of an apprentice of Jesus—being with him, becoming like him, and doing as he did—aren't strict stages, the main imperative is to always return to being with him, for the whole of our spiritual lives flows from our communion with God, or what John, the beloved disciple, calls "abiding." Only when we learn to truly abide in Jesus do we begin to grasp what Paul talks about in today's Scripture: the vast, deep, wide, and long love of God for us.

To set the stage for the final conversation of this Practice, here are a few beautiful words from Ronald Rolhesier on this way of praying:

> You must try to pray so that, in your prayer, you open yourself in such
> a way that sometime—perhaps not today, but sometime—you are
> able to hear God say to you, "I love you!" . . . Before you hear [these
> words], nothing is ever completely right with you, but, after you hear
> them, something will be right in your life at a very deep level.*

---

* "Affective Prayer," Ron Rolheiser, accessed April 8, 2025, at ronrolheiser.com/affective-prayer/.

Read Ephesians 3v16—19

Discuss the Scripture

01   Pause and have one person slowly pray these words over the group. Afterward, discuss what aspects of the prayer captured you most, and why.

02   Would you say you rely on believing God's love for you more through knowledge or experience? Why do you think that is?

03   The experience of God's love feels very real for some, elusive for others, and can change from season to season. What has this looked like in your own life?

04   What from this Scripture feels missing in your life right now? What invitation do you sense there?

Discuss the practice

01   What did your time in contemplative prayer look like this week?

02   How much time did you choose to spend in this form of prayer? How did you experience distraction during this time? What did you notice happening in you as time went on?

03   Consider the different forms and practices of prayer you have tried throughout this Practice. Which of these left an impression on you? How do you imagine integrating them into your life of prayer going forward?

C4   If you could share only one insight or reflection that you want to internalize going forward from this Practice, what would it be?

Repeat the exercise

For this final week, we invite you to continue in the practice of contemplative prayer. This time, reflect on last week's experience and consider how you might want to change your posture, environment, or the words or phrases you repeat.

We also encourage you, as you wrap up this Practice, to take time to review each of the session exercises, as well as your practice reflections, and prayerfully decide how you plan to integrate these different prayers and practices into your life of prayer.

What would an ideal but doable rhythm of daily prayer look like for you going forward? Write your plan below.

APPENDIX

Recommended Prayers

Make Me an Instrument of Your Peace

Saint Francis of Assisi

Lord, make me an instrument of your peace.

Where there is hatred, let me sow love;

where there is injury, pardon;

where there is doubt, faith;

where there is despair, hope;

where there is darkness, light;

and where there is sadness, joy.

O Divine Master, grant that I may not so much seek

to be consoled as to console;

to be understood as to understand;

to be loved as to love.

For it is in giving that we receive;

it is in pardoning that we are pardoned;

and it is in dying that we are born to eternal life.

Amen.

The Serenity Prayer*

God grant me the serenity
To accept the things I cannot change;
Courage to change the things I can;
And wisdom to know the difference.
Living one day at a time;
Enjoying one moment at a time;
Accepting hardships as the pathway to peace;
Taking, as He did, this sinful world
As it is, not as I would have it;
Trusting that He will make all things right
If I surrender to His Will;
So that I may be reasonably happy in this life
And supremely happy with Him
Forever and ever in the next.

Amen.

*Likely composed by theologian Reinhold Niebuhr
but popularized by Alcoholics Anonymous*

Guidance Prayer
Saint Teresa of Ávila

Lord,

grant that I may always allow myself to be guided by You,

always follow Your plans,

and perfectly accomplish Your Holy Will.

Grant that in all things, great and small,

today and all the days of my life,

I may do whatever You require of me.

Help me respond to the slightest prompting of Your Grace,

so that I may be Your trustworthy instrument for Your honor.

May Your Will be done in time and in eternity by me,

in me, and through me.

Amen.

Bookmark Prayer*
Saint Teresa of Ávila

Let nothing disturb you;

Let nothing frighten you.

All things are passing.

God never changes.

Patience obtains all things.

Nothing is wanting to him who possesses God.

God alone suffices.

**Named "Bookmark Prayer" because it was found on a handwritten
bookmark upon her death*

Breastplate Prayer

Saint Patrick

I arise today
Through a mighty strength, the invocation of the Trinity,
Through belief in the Threeness,
Through confession of the Oneness
of the Creator of creation.

I arise today
Through the strength of Christ's birth with His baptism,
Through the strength of His crucifixion with His burial,
Through the strength of His resurrection with His ascension,
Through the strength of His descent for the judgment of doom.

I arise today
Through the strength of the love of cherubim,
In the obedience of angels,
In the service of archangels,
In the hope of resurrection to meet with reward,
In the prayers of patriarchs,
In the predictions of prophets,
In the preaching of apostles,
In the faith of confessors,
In the innocence of holy virgins,
In the deeds of righteous men.

I arise today, through
The strength of heaven,
The light of the sun,
The radiance of the moon,
The splendor of fire,
The speed of lightning,

The swiftness of wind,
The depth of the sea,
The stability of the earth,
The firmness of rock.

I arise today, through
God's strength to pilot me,
God's might to uphold me,
God's wisdom to guide me,
God's eye to look before me,
God's ear to hear me,
God's word to speak for me,
God's hand to guard me,
God's shield to protect me,
God's host to save me
From snares of devils,
From temptation of vices,
From everyone who shall wish me ill,
afar and near.

I summon today
All these powers between me and those evils,
Against every cruel and merciless power
that may oppose my body and soul,
Against incantations of false prophets,
Against black laws of pagandom,
Against false laws of heretics,
Against craft of idolatry,
Against spells of witches and smiths and wizards,
Against every knowledge that corrupts man's body and soul;
Christ to shield me today
Against poison, against burning,

Against drowning, against wounding,

So that there may come to me an abundance of reward.

Christ with me,

Christ before me,

Christ behind me,

Christ in me,

Christ beneath me,

Christ above me,

Christ on my right,

Christ on my left,

Christ when I lie down,

Christ when I sit down,

Christ when I arise,

Christ in the heart of every man who thinks of me,

Christ in the mouth of everyone who speaks of me,

Christ in every eye that sees me,

Christ in every ear that hears me.

I arise today

Through a mighty strength, the invocation of the Trinity,

Through belief in the Threeness,

Through confession of the Oneness

of the Creator of creation.

PRAYERS FOR THE HOURS

Strahan Coleman, from *Prayer Vol. 02*

As the dawning light ascends, God,
so do I to You,
so do I in You,
to the melody of Your love.

Today is Yours, Father,
and as with every day,
You have made it ours.
So may my steps be as Your steps,
my words be as Your words,
and my heart be as Your heart,
until the dusk arrives
to beckon me to rest once more.

Strahan Coleman, from *Prayer Vol. 02*

We are with ourselves here in the dark, Father,
aware of our vulnerabilities,
our needs and mortal limitations.
All we have done today is now left to rest in You,
or grow in You,
depending on Your will.
We have done all we could,
yet perhaps not all we should.
We trust You now as always, God,
with both.

Meet us as we sleep, so our souls—
our hearts—will wake with new
energy for greater love.
You will never leave us,
not in the day,
and now not in the night.
We trust in You with all our greatest
love and hope.

Prayer for Mission
From the Book of Common Prayer

Keep watch, dear Lord, with those who work, or watch, or weep this night, and give your angels charge over those who sleep. Tend the sick, Lord Christ; give rest to the weary, bless the dying, soothe the suffering, pity the afflicted, shield the joyous; and all for your love's sake.

Amen.

0/ /4

✓

To inquire about ordering this Companion Guide in
bulk quantities for your church, small group, or staff,
contact churches@penguinrandomhouse.com.